Vegetables

Julia Adams

WAYLAND

Explore the world with **Popcorn** – your complete first non-fiction library.

Look out for more titles in the Popcorn range. All books have the same format of simple text and striking images. Text is carefully matched to the pictures to help readers to identify and understand key vocabulary.
www.waylandbooks.co.uk/popcorn

First published in 2010 by Wayland
Copyright © Wayland 2010

This paperback edition published in 2012 by Wayland.

Wayland
Hachette Children's Books
338 Euston Road
London NW1 3BH

Wayland Australia
Level 17/207 Kent Street
Sydney NSW 2000

Editor: Julia Adams
Managing Editor: Victoria Brooker
Designer: Paul Cherrill
Picture Researcher: Julia Adams
Food and Nutrition Consultant: Ester Davies
Photo Models: Asha Francis; Lydia Washbourne

British Library Cataloguing in Publication Data
Adams, Julia.
   Vegetables. -- (Popcorn. Good food)
   1. Vegetables--Juvenile literature. 2. Vegetables in
      human nutrition--Juvenile literature.
   I. Title II. Series
   641.3'5-dc22
ISBN 978 0 7502 6760 1

Wayland is a division of Hachette Children's Books,
an Hachette UK company.
www.hachette.co.uk

Photographs:

Alamy: David Wootton 9, Johner Images 12, Bon Appetit 15; Andy Crawford: 20, 22, 23; Corbis: AgStock Images 8; Getty: Dorling Kindersley 19; iStock: PerkerDeen OFC/7, wyndy25 10, nojustice 14; Shutterstock: margouillat photo 1/6, 3dfoto 2/18, Monkey Business Images 4/5/13/17/21, siamionau pavel 11, luchschen 16;

Contents

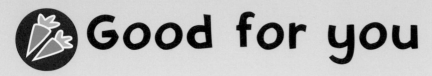# Good for you

Everyone needs to eat the right kind of food to stay healthy. The food we eat comes from plants and animals.

Many dishes, such as salad and stir-fry, are made with vegetables.

Vegetables are good for us. They have a lot of vitamins and minerals. Our bodies need vitamins and minerals to stay healthy.

Carrots contain vitamin A, which is good for your eyes.

Vegetables contain fibre. This helps our bodies to get rid of unwanted food.

5

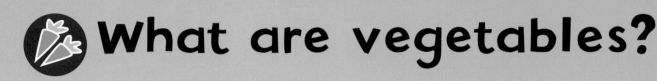

What are vegetables?

Vegetables are parts of plants that we use as food. Some vegetables are the roots of a plant. Others are the leaves or stems.

Can you name any of these vegetables?

Some vegetables need to be cooked before we can eat them. Vegetables like spinach and lettuce can be eaten raw.

What are your favourite vegetables?

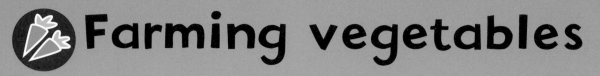 # Farming vegetables

Many of the vegetables we eat are grown on farms. The farmer plants rows of vegetables in big fields.

These beans are planted in rows, so they can be picked easily.

Harvest time is when vegetables are ready to be picked. Most farmers use machines for picking vegetables.

This machine is picking beans from a field.

H984 VVF

FMC

Root vegetables

Some plants grow very thick roots. We eat many of these roots as vegetables. Carrots, parsnips, turnips and beetroot are root vegetables.

These parsnips have just been harvested. Can you see the soil?

We eat some root vegetables raw. Many root vegetables can also be made into soups.

Do you know any vegetables that are made into soup?

 # Tubers

Some plants have stems that swell up underground. These parts of the plant are called tubers. Potatoes and yams are tubers.

Can you see the potatoes that have just been pulled out of the ground?

We need to cook tubers before we can eat them. We can boil, mash, bake or fry them. We fry potatoes to make chips.

A baked potato with salad makes a delicious lunch.

Plants grow tubers to store food for the winter.

13

 # Flowers

Broccoli and cauliflower grow at the top of plant stems. They are the flower buds of these plants.

We eat the buds of broccoli plants. If they aren't picked in time, they start blossoming!

We usually cook flower vegetables. We eat them as a side dish or in soups, bakes and quiches.

This dish is called cauliflower cheese. Do you know why?

 Leaves and stems

Vegetables such as spinach, lettuce and cabbage are the leaves of plants. We eat a lot of leaf vegetables raw.

This is a savoy cabbage. Its leaves are big, thick and rubbery.

We sometimes eat the stems of plants, too. Asparagus and celery are stem vegetables.

We often eat celery in salads or as a snack.

Legumes and pulses

Peas, beans and lentils are seeds that grow in pods. When they are fresh, we call them legumes. When they are dried, we call them pulses.

Can you see the peas growing inside the pod?

Soya beans are used to make tofu. You can eat tofu instead of meat.

Legumes can be eaten raw, but pulses always need to be cooked before we can eat them.

Many Indian dishes, such as dhal, are made with pulses.

Fruit vegetables

Fruits are the fleshy part of a plant that have seeds inside. Most fruits are sweet. The ones that are not are eaten as vegetables.

Can you see the seeds in these fruit vegetables?

Cucumbers, peppers, tomatoes and pumpkins are all fruit vegetables. Many fruit vegetables can be eaten raw. They are often added to salads.

Which fruit vegetables are in this salad?

Make a hummus dip

Follow these steps to make some delicious hummus. You can eat it with carrots and celery as a snack.

1. Drain the chickpeas and add them to the bowl.

2. Ask an adult to peel and chop a clove of garlic. Add it to the bowl, together with one tablespoon of tahini.

3. Ask an adult to cut a lemon in half. Add the juice of half the lemon to the bowl.

4. Add four tablespoons of olive oil to the bowl. Mix everything with a spoon.

5. Add salt and pepper. Use a fork to mash the mixture until it is smooth.

6. Wash the carrots and celery. Cut them into sticks.

7. You can eat the hummus with the celery and carrot sticks. Enjoy!

BETTWS 17/2/2012

Glossary

fruit the soft, fleshy part of a plant that holds the seeds

minerals substances in food that keep our bodies healthy. Calcium is a mineral that helps to build strong bones.

pod a long, fleshy case that peas or beans grow in

raw not cooked

root the part of a plant that grows beneath the ground

seeds parts of plants that grow to form new plants

vitamins substances in food that help keep our bodies healthy and stop us from catching colds

Index